THE GOOD NEWS

Jesus Christ and Him Crucified

ZECHARIAH ANDERSON

D0488769

The Good News: Jesus Christ and Him Crucified (Paperback edition)
ISBN: 9798736775699
Copyright © ImmanuelMinistries.org

TABLE OF CONTENTS

THE INTRODUCTION

God has not forgotten about you. He knows exactly who you are, where you are, and what you are going through. You are not living by accident; God has made you for a reason.

There is more to this life than meets the eye—a whole unseen realm, a spiritual world, and a constant battle going on between good and evil, right and wrong; and there are two different ways we can live our lives, each way with their own end destination: God's way (leading to eternal life) or the world's way (leading to eternal destruction). *Which way are you living?*

The good news is that you can overcome evil, have peace with God, and have an intimate, loving relationship with Him that lasts forever if you are willing to wholeheartedly place your faith in Jesus Christ, believing in who He is and what He's done.

Who is Jesus Christ? What has He done? And what is God's way of living? you may be wondering... This book is written to answer these questions and give an insight into key Christian teachings; may it broaden your understanding and be a useful Bible-based resource to bring you closer to God.

THE CREATOR

God is the Creator of all things. He is the First and the Last—no-one came before Him and no-one will be after Him. He is perfect in every way. He is everywhere, and He is not held back by anything or anyone. He never changes and is in charge as the Righteous Judge over all of creation.

We are not able to see, sense, or understand all the wonderful ways in which God works, but if we seek Him, learn about Him, and come to know Him personally, things will be made clearer and more of His character will be revealed to us—for instance, we will learn more about His infinite wisdom, His abounding love, His almighty power, His attention to detail, and His no-nonsense approach to getting things done.

There is only one God, yet He co-eternally exists in three distinct forms: He is the Father, the Son (Jesus Christ), and the Holy Spirit. All three are fully God, yet are in different forms to make up the Godhead—which is more widely known as the Trinity. Another way to describe the Trinity is that God is one essence and three persons. Each member has the same desires and carry out their own specific roles in perfect harmony with one another. Understanding both God's tri-unity and His oneness is hard for us because His holy nature is unique compared to anything in the world.

The ways in which God works are majestic, mysterious, and unfathomable to us. If we knew all the ins and outs of everything in our lives, and how the pieces of our puzzles fit together, there would be no need for faith because we would be like God. There will always be a gap between our abilities and God's abilities—that is the way He created us—however, when people choose to place their faith in Jesus Christ, they become connected with God and are transformed into new creations who can tap into His power by the indwelling of the Holy Spirit.

Faith is believing in what we cannot see or prove, and we all apply our faith every single day. For instance, people may believe what the weather forecast says; they may believe that a meal in a restaurant is safe to eat; or, they may believe that the brakes on their car work effectively.

When people commit their lives to God, their decision is made by faith; they will believe in these things: God is who He says He is, God is true to His Word, and God is absolutely perfect in every way.

THE ENEMY

The world is a spiritual war zone and the dangers around us are real yet so often get unnoticed or underestimated. The evil power behind the trouble and torment in this world is the devil—who is also known as Satan, the enemy, the deceiver, and the father of lies.

Even though terribly bad things happen in the world, there is nothing outside of God's control and nothing that He has not allowed to happen—everything works according to His plan. This can be challenging for some people as they may question God's goodness and why He allows so much suffering. We may not be sure of the reasons, but we can be sure that He does know the reasons and that He is the One to go to if we want to be able to overcome the trials that we encounter in our lives.

Satan steals, kills, and destroys. He aims to harm everyone and everything good that God has made. He aims to poison our minds with negativity, derail us from living morally upright lives, and disrupt our relationships with God. He aims to lead us into hell—the place of punishment, darkness, and eternal destruction.

In the same way that God has angels working for good, Satan has demons working for evil, who wage war against all of God's goodness.

THE PEOPLE

God made the world and everything in it—absolutely everything, including the tiniest insects to the tallest mountains. He made Adam and Eve, who were the first two humans, and put them in a place called the Garden of Eden. They were given the responsibilities of tending to the garden, populating the earth, and ruling over every living creature.

Humans were created in God's image—in a way that resembled Him and could connect with Him, think rationally, and sense what is right and wrong. All was very good indeed, but Satan came onto the scene and things took a turn for the worse.

THE FALL

Satan—in the form of a snake—tricked Adam and Eve into disobeying God by eating from the Tree of Knowledge, even though this was the one thing God told them not to do. By this immoral act, sin entered into the world, which led to the corruption of the natural world as well as human nature.

Subsequently, the ground became cursed, suffering began, and the original powers that God gave mankind were stripped from them and passed onto Satan—making him the ruler of this world. These events are known as the Fall. Sin then stood in the way between God and mankind. In order for the relationship to be restored, sin had to be removed in some way and people had to be redeemed. God knew exactly how it was going to happen and how He was going to make it happen.

Because Adam and Eve acted wickedly, God decided to banish them from the Garden of Eden. To this day, the world has been full of pain and problems because Satan continues to cause trouble and because the selfish, sinful nature within Adam and Eve continues to be passed onto the rest of mankind.

Therefore, even though we may try and live good, moral, upright lives, we are all guilty before God and fall short of His standards because of our sins and because we have the desire to sin ingrained in our fallen human form. Even Christian believers—who are freed from the bondage of sin—still displease God and do not live sinless lives; but as they mature in faith, they become more aware of their sin and more able to act faithfully and defeat their temptations.

THE FLOOD

Many years after the Fall, God was deeply grieved about the way in which people were living, so much so, that He intervened and essentially pressed the earth's 'reset button' by sending a great flood to wipe clean the whole earth.

However, preceding the flood, a good man named Noah found favor with God. Noah was told by God to make a big wooden boat to protect him, his family, and each form of living creature from the flood that was coming. Even though Noah looked foolish to the world, he faithfully did exactly what God told him to do, and it was a good job he did.

God sent a torrential downpour of rain which lasted for forty days and forty nights; it destroyed every living thing that was left on the face of the earth. The inhabitants of the boat survived the flood as intended, and over time, the earth became repopulated by them. God promised never to do this again and rainbows are given to us as a beautiful, symbolic reminder of this promise.

THE COMMANDMENTS

Several hundred years later, God chose a man called Abraham and his wife Sarah to start a new race of people—called the Israelites—who were to live in a way that honored Him. Abraham was a man of faith, and God blessed him, not because of his obedience, but because of his faith. Even though Abraham and Sarah were very old, God enabled them to have a son, named Isaac. The Israelites grew greatly in number.

Many years later, a man from Abraham's descendants, named Moses, was chosen by God to lead the Israelites out of Egypt and free them from the captivity they were under at that time. God helped the Israelites by sending ten plagues on the Egyptians and by parting the Red Sea. Pharaoh's army chased the Israelites with horsemen, chariots, and horsemen. God instructed Moses to raise his hand over the sea, and this caused the waters to sweep over Pharaoh' army, causing them all to die. When the Israelites saw the amazing things that God had done for them, and how He had delivered them, they were filled with awe. They put their trust in Him and His servant Moses.

Later on, God summoned Moses up a mountain to give him Ten Commandments—along with other Laws—for the Israelites to follow. These were given to Moses so that the Israelites could know practically how to live in a way that pleased God, protected them, and would cause them and their descendants to prosper. To this day, the Ten Commandments are still important for Christians to try to live by—even though Jesus fulfilled them in His life on their behalf.

Here are the Ten Commandments[1]:

1. Have no other gods before Me (put God first).
2. Do not make idols (only worship God).
3. Do not take the name of the Lord your God in vain (do not disrespect God and sacred things with your words).
4. Keep the Sabbath day holy (set aside a holy day of worship and rest each week).
5. Honor your parents (love, respect, and help your parents).
6. Do not murder (do not kill others).
7. Do not commit adultery (be loyal to your spouse).
8. Do not steal (Do not take what is not yours without permission).
9. Do not bear false witness against your neighbor (do not speak wrongly about other people and lie).
10. Do not covet (do not be jealous of what other people have).

Back then, sacrificial offerings had to be made to God to pay the debt for the times when people acted immorally. In the Bible, it is written that the shedding of blood is necessary for there to be forgiveness of sins—God takes disobedience very seriously.

Over a thousand years after the Commandments and Laws were given, sinful living was spreading like wildfire and the world was in a bad state once again: even many of the Israelites became conformed to the world and got tired of doing what they were told to do. It was time for God to bring the next phase of His plan of redemption into action.

THE SAVIOR

We can be thankful that God did not cast everyone into hell. Instead, He showed His mercy by sending a Lifeline: He Himself came onto the earth in the flesh, in the form of Jesus Christ. God did this so that whoever believes in Him will be forgiven of their sins, be counted as righteous (morally upright and pure), and become a member of God's family forever.

Jesus was both truly God and truly man during His time on earth. He knew what lay before Him, including all the immense suffering that He would have to endure to set His people free. He knew what it was going to cost Him to complete His task: it was going to cost Him His life.

Jesus' life story was foretold before it happened. Over the years, God spoke to several people—known as Prophets—and their written accounts are documented in the Old Testament section in the Bible. Before Jesus was born, many people were living with a hope of an expected 'Messiah' who was written about—He was the One who would come to save them from their sins. Jesus was exactly the promised Messiah they were hoping for, yet many people were unaware of this, even though He dwelled among them, fulfilled certain prophecies, and performed many signs and wonders.

God made His entry into the world as a baby—born in such modest circumstances—as opposed to appearing as the mighty kingly figure who many people were expecting. God chose a young, faithful lady called Mary to be Jesus' mother. She was a virgin and was engaged to be married to a man called Joseph. Mary and Joseph made a long journey to Bethlehem on a donkey, and it was there where Jesus was born.

Jesus' birth is celebrated at Christmas, and God's love, peace, and joy are key themes within the festivities. One of Jesus' names is Immanuel, which means 'God with us'.

Shepherds and three wise men came to witness Jesus' birth. The shepherds were instructed by an angel where to go, and the wise men followed a big star that directed them. These people were led to an animal stable where Jesus was born. They were able to witness this momentous, glorious occasion.

God showed love for His people by shining His Light into this dark world. Jesus is the Light of the world who overcomes all darkness; and He enables people to overcome the darkness in their lives and shine brightly themselves, through believing in Him.

Throughout Jesus' time on earth, He lived a perfect, sinless life. He lived as a Jew in a place called Nazareth in Galilee, Israel, and grew up following in Joseph's footsteps by becoming a carpenter in His early adulthood.

There was a man called John the Baptist who was a forerunner to Jesus. He was preparing people for the coming Messiah (Jesus). He baptized (immersed) people in the River Jordan to symbolize their faith in the coming Messiah and the cleansing process of their sins being forgiven. John was telling people to repent of their sins (show sorrow for their sins and commit to turn from them) because the Kingdom of Heaven was near.[2]

One day, Jesus went to John and asked to be baptized by him. John felt unworthy to do such a thing, but after some encouragement, he followed through and did it. As soon as Jesus came out of the water, the heavens opened and the Holy Spirit—in the form of a dove—descended and rested on Him; a voice from heaven then said, "This is My beloved Son, in whom I am well pleased!"[3]

After Jesus was baptized, He was immediately led by the Holy Spirit into the wilderness where He fasted for forty days and forty nights. It was there where He was tempted by Satan. Satan tried to get Jesus to worship him, perform miracles to feed Himself, and to see if angels would save Him if He were to jump from the top of a temple. Jesus overcame all of these temptations and rebuked Satan by quoting Bible passages back at him. This caused Satan to leave Jesus. Angels then came to minister to Jesus.

When Jesus was around thirty years of age, His Ministry began. In Galilee, back where He grew up, Jesus preached in synagogues and gathered some followers—known as His disciples—who joined Him on His journey that would change the future of the world forever.

THE MISSION

Jesus and His disciples went from city to city telling people about God. They were sharing God's teachings, performing miracles, casting out evil spirits, and healing the sick. The Word of God was spreading rapidly, and more people were becoming increasingly excited as they came to believe that Jesus was indeed the Messiah who was written about in the Old Testament. Jesus was creating a following, and hope grew amongst the people.

Jesus and His disciples arrived in Jerusalem, which was where the religious leaders were based and where Jesus was destined to be sacrificed. The religious leaders were offended and threatened by Jesus so they plotted against Him—with the help of Jesus' disloyal follower named Judas. Jesus was accused by the religious leaders of several things, such as blaspheming against God and not resting on the set apart holy day—the Sabbath.

In Jesus' Ministry, He emphasized the seriousness of sin and revealed how sinful people really are. He 'ramped up' the meaning of the Commandments and said bold statements such as, '... anyone who looks at a woman to lust after her has already committed adultery with her in his heart';[4] and '... if someone is angry at someone else—without cause—they are subject to judgement'.[5] Many people were self-deceived into thinking that they were on the right track—by sticking to the Scriptures and following religious rituals to the finest detail—but Jesus gave them and the rest of the world a startling reality check. He shared the message that God likes to see humility and kind-heartedness, not self-righteousness and hard-hearted religiosity.

A revolutionary teaching that Jesus shared with people was that the two greatest Commandments were these: (1) to '... love the Lord your God with all your heart and with all your soul and with all your mind and with all your strength'[6]; and (2) to '... love your neighbor as yourself'.[7] Together these Commandments form the 'gold standard' of Christian behavior, and they emphasize that Christians can obey all the biblical teachings through loving others with a love that is grounded in their faith in God and their devotion to Him.

Jesus' teachings and actions were causing a stir, and the religious leaders did what they could to put a stop to all the controversy. Little did they know that the proceedings were all planned in advance by God and were in fact fulfilling prophecies from the biblical Scriptures.

Jesus was taken, trialed before the rulers, and then sentenced to death by way of crucifixion. He was brutally tortured and ridiculed before being nailed to a cross and then left to die. Crucifixion is one of the most barbaric ways to be killed imaginable. Jesus willingly underwent this immense suffering which displays His inner-strength, humility, loyalty to His Father, and love for His people. On the cross, Jesus said, "It is finished"[8] to announce the culmination of His mission—His victory over evil, the fulfillment of the Law, the end of His suffering, and the redemption of His people.

There were several signs and wonders that took place when Jesus died, such as an earthquake, the sun going dark, and a big curtain in the Temple being torn in two—which could symbolize several things, such as God's anger at sin, the end of the old sacrificial system, the breaking of Jesus' body, and the breaking of the barrier of sin that stood between God and His believers.

After Jesus died, He was placed in a tomb, and three days later He miraculously arose from the dead, whereby He defeated evil, death, and the power of sin. Ever since then, whoever believes in Him can be delivered from the dominion of darkness and be brought into His Kingdom.

As well as being the King of kings in His Kingdom, Jesus is the biggest Servant of all; He humbled Himself to the point of willingly sacrificing Himself to pay the price for the sins of His people and thereby make them justified before God (just as if they had never sinned), even though they deserve eternal punishment for their sins and He lived a totally sinless life.

It is by God's grace (His undeserved favor and divine enabling power), and through faith, that believers can receive forgiveness and have Christ's righteousness (His moral uprightness) 'credited into their accounts'—they can receive Jesus' perfect record despite the fact that they themselves deserve nothing but hell.

Jesus lived a perfect life and died on the cross, and in doing so, He fulfilled the old Laws and Commandments and became the Ultimate Sacrifice which consequently put an end to believers having to make sin offerings—like animal sacrifices—to God in order to receive forgiveness and please God.

Jesus is referred to as both the 'Lamb of God'[9] who has been slain and the conquering 'Lion of Judah'.[10] The Lamb of God title can symbolize His gentleness, innocence, and His substitutional, sacrificial death; and the Lion of Judah can symbolize His boldness, strength, and deadly power, as well as symbolize the prophecies concerning His human bloodline and His eternal victory as King.

God knows what it is like to endure hardship. He knows what it is like to be persecuted. He has shown compassion for His people: Jesus went into darkness so believers could go into the light; He was punished so they could be pardoned; He died so they could live; He redeemed His believers with His precious blood.

God is merciful, fair, and faithful. He is love.

THE GOSPEL

The restored relationship between God and His believers is the most amazing gift, and this relationship relies on these things: grace, faith, and Christ—the grace of God, a believer's faith in Christ, and the identity and works of Christ. These things are fundamental components that bring about salvation and form the heart of what is known as the Gospel.

If you 'profess' faith and 'possess' faith, you will be saved: the Bible says that 'if you confess with your mouth, "Jesus is Lord," and believe in your heart that God raised Him from the dead, you will be saved"[11]; and in being saved, you will have your 'slate' wiped clean of sin, be united with God, inherit eternal life, and—in this life—be able to work with the Holy Spirit and grow in holiness as you are continually transformed from the inside out by Him. This is the Gospel, the good news, the success story of Jesus Christ, the cross, and His resurrection.

Moreover, believers choose to worship and offer their lives as a living sacrifice to the Lord, in homage to all that He is and all that He has done, still does, and will do for them.

Not only did Jesus live a perfect life and die as the perfect Sacrifice; He miraculously arose from the dead. He is not dead; He has risen, and His believers will rise as well. This news is what gives believers so much inner-strength. Due to their faith and God's grace, nothing in their lives can ultimately defeat them once them they have been saved by Christ—not even death.

Faith in Christ is the only remedy for sin; faith in Him is the only way to be forgiven; and faith in Him is the only way to be freed from facing God's wrath (His intense anger). Jesus Christ Himself said that He is the Way, the Truth, and the Life and that no one comes to the Father except through Him.[12] Jesus is not simply a way to God; He is God, and the Gospel bears witness to the Truth and the weightiness of His, life, death, and resurrection.

The newness of life that Jesus made available for believers is celebrated at Easter. In addition, believers regularly partake in Holy Communion—also known as the Lord's Supper—to acknowledge the significance of Jesus' sacrificial death which accounted for their sins. Holy Communion is where bread and—most commonly—wine are consumed to represent Jesus' body which was broken and His blood which was shed. Holy Communion is also a way of commemorating the last meal that Jesus had with His disciples before He was crucified.

After Jesus' resurrection, over a period of forty days, He appeared to His disciples on several occasions in His resurrected body. He proved to them that He had indeed risen from the grave and was more than a mere figment of their imagination: He walked and talked with them, ate with them, and even got one of His doubtful disciples to feel the wounds on His body. He commanded His disciples to share His teachings to the whole world and to preach the Gospel to every creature.

The Gospel will be shared and heard worldwide in one way or another. And the opportunity to be made right with God is available to whoever turns to Him and believes in what He has done through Jesus Christ. Jesus came to offer life to people, not to punish them.

And to be able to receive salvation, things such as skin color or social status are irrelevant and do not matter in the slightest: salvation depends on the spiritual condition of the heart, and whether or not people trust God with their lives and believe in the Gospel.

THE HELPER

Before the mass sharing of God's teachings took place, Jesus told His disciples to wait in Jerusalem for a Gift they were going to receive; He was referring to the Holy Spirit who was to come. The Holy Spirit is also referred to as the Advocate; He is God's Power who acts as the Helper and Comforter to believers.

Shortly after giving His instructions to the disciples, Jesus ascended into heaven to take His place beside His Father as the King of kings and the Lord of lords—where He still is to this day carrying out His role of interceding for His people.

As promised, after Jesus' ascension to heaven, the Holy Spirit entered the bodies of His disciples to equip them with the supernatural power they required for their assigned responsibility of sharing all the good news to the world. This day is remembered as the Day of Pentecost. The message of good news began to be shared across all nations, and this was the start of the Christian Church movement under the New Covenant (the promise of salvation made available by God's grace and through faith in Christ's sacrificial death and victorious resurrection).

All people who receive Jesus Christ as their Lord and Savior by faith have the Holy Spirit living inside them. God extends His grace to them, and the indwelling of the Holy Spirit gives them a totally new way of life that is better than they could ever have hoped for or imagined. They become spiritually 'born-again'.

Water baptisms are when believers are sprinkled with water or dipped under water to symbolize the washing away of their sins and the new life they have in union with God. Water baptisms tend to be done by believers who want to express their commitment to God, although some believers choose to have their infant children baptized. Water baptisms can also be called 'christenings' and different groups of believers have different views and approaches to these things.

There are baptisms—also known as 'fillings'—of the Holy Spirit where He supernaturally pours into believers to provide them with what they need at the time to live a devoted, godly life; for instance, He helps them fulfill their Christian duties and defends them against evil. God is always with believers as their ever-present Helper and Refuge, and the Holy Spirit is given to them as a Guarantee of their salvation and of their heavenly inheritance.

As believers get closer to God, the Holy Spirit grows godly characteristics in them, such as love, joy, peace, patience, kindness, goodness, faithfulness, gentleness, and self-control (known as fruits of the Spirit), which make them more effective representatives of Jesus in the world and allow them to flourish in their lives and show God's greatness.

We can see in the Bible that interactions with the Holy Spirit can happen at different times along a person's spiritual journey with God, and these events do not necessarily happen in the same way for everyone. God gives His people what they need at the right time; He knows what is best for them.

Gifts of the Holy Spirit are given to believers. These gifts are special talents and abilities that help believers serve God better and carry out His plans for their lives. The Bible clearly states that God encourages believers to ask to receive the gifts of the Spirit.

God, through the Holy Spirit, still works miraculously in the world today; and He works in and through His people as a method of bringing about miracles and bringing His plans to pass. The standpoint on the degree of supernatural abilities and gifts that believers can inherit—in comparison to biblical times—differs within certain branches of Christianity.

The benefits that Jesus has earned for believers are given to them through the Holy Spirit. The Spirit plays a vital role in the Gospel—as He does with everything. Believers were dead in sin—like the rest of the world—before they came to faith in Christ and chose to follow Him. The Spirit gives life.[13]

THE AFTERLIFE

People who are 'saved'—who are counted as righteous before God —gain the privilege of living with God in this life and for eternity. In the future, believers get to enjoy dwelling in the fullness of God's presence, away from death, crying, and pain. God has prepared and stored up amazing things for those who love Him.

In the future, believers will be rewarded with eternal treasures in accordance with how they have lived in their bodies; also, they will receive imperishable bodies, like that of Jesus' resurrected body.

Eternal life in God's Kingdom is an amazing blessing that encourages believers and fills them with hope. Also, seeing their Lord and Savior face to face is something that they are very much looking forward to. These things make any hardships that believers encounter in their current earthly lives a lot easier to bear; they know that their hardships are no comparison to the everlasting joy that awaits them in the future when they get to witness the revealing of God's glory and gaze upon His beauty.

On the other hand, people who reject God—who do not turn to Him and receive Jesus as their Lord and Savior—will face judgment and be punished for eternity. God does not take sin lightly; He judges fairly and punishes bad behavior. He has set the standards, and He has the authority to bring to justice whoever does not stick to those standards—and that includes non-believing people who seem to live decent lives.

In the Bible, the events surrounding the 'end times' and Jesus' return are written about in prophecies. These prophecies can be interpreted in different ways, and Christians have different views on how these prophecies will all come to pass. However, regardless of whichever standpoint Christians have, they can be sure that Christ is King, He will return in power and glory, people will be judged, evil will be defeated forever, and they will have eternal life with Him.

Believers are encouraged by these promises, and Jesus' return could happen at any particular time. Also, the hard truth is that each of us could die at any particular time; therefore, with these points in mind, if we want to be forgiven, have peace with God, and inherit eternal life, we cannot reject God or simply 'sit on the fence' of Christianity—with a lukewarm faith—but instead, we need to humble ourselves and make the most out of our lives by fully committing ourselves to Him while we still can. This is why believers are taught to live ever ready, in a way that respects their Savior and represents their salvation.

THE IDOLS

An idol is something or someone that is worshipped (loved, cherished, and valued) more than God. God commands that He should be worshipped first and foremost in people's lives and that nothing or no one should take His spot. The Bible stresses the dangers of idolatry, stating that idolators will not inherit the Kingdom of God.[14]

Whatever we place higher than God in our lives trap us, control us, and consume us. Many people place so much emphasis on things like appearances, power, sensual pleasures, possessions, education, entertainment, and popularity—these sorts of things become their gods. It is sad to say, but we are all guilty of allowing worldly things to become our idols; whenever we sin, we are putting our desires above God's desires and we are essentially worshipping a false god. If we want to honor God, be at peace with Him, and truly live the best lives, we need to humble ourselves: we need to set aside our self-righteous pride and set our sights on God, remembering that without Him we would have nothing, we would not be able to do anything, and we would not even be alive.

God has blessed us with great things to enjoy, but if we place our faith in worldly things and they happen to be taken away from us, our lives would seemingly fall apart and we would lose our peace and our whole sense of purpose. This is because we would be living for God's creations rather than Him—the Creator; we would be disrespecting Him who is the Source, the Provider, the stable Rock, and we would be building our lives upon 'faulty foundations', playing into the hands of Satan.

Worldly things can only bring us temporary satisfaction; they can seem on the surface as though they will be the answer to all of our problems, yet in reality, when they replace God and are misused, they cause serious problems: lives are wasted, defiled, or even lost over them. Nothing can satisfy us deep down like God can, and sinful living can seem great but it only leads to disappointment and eternal doom—it has to be dealt with.

Life is precious, and sadly, so many people spend so much time and effort chasing things that one day they will regret; they will see that they have invested in worthless, meaningless things. People can spend their whole lives trying to find satisfaction in their sins; they can listen to the lies of the world, and be caught up in an immoral, crooked culture, without ever coming to know, love, and trust their Maker—the only true God.

However, if we have God as the Treasure we worship and live for, we will have a Treasure that can never be taken away from us: we will be secure; we will be satisfied; we will be able to rely on His strength; we will be able to stand strong in faith throughout all the challenging circumstances that come our way; and we will be investing in our salvation.

Christians are taught to have a holy, restful day of worship each week called the Sabbath. For most Christians, this is on a Sunday and usually involves going to church and spending high-quality time focusing on God. Setting aside one day a week, not only provides believers rest from their work, but it also allows them to make sure that their priorities are in order—with God at the top, where He should be.

In addition, Christians are taught to fast, which is a practice where they discipline themselves by temporarily abstaining from things like foods at certain times. Fasting has many benefits: when it is done properly it can break and prevent addictions and idolatry; humble us before God; help us hear from Him more clearly; maintain and restore a healthy, balanced lifestyle; cause us to count our blessings; and cause spiritual breakthroughs. Fasting usually accompanies praying and is very much a private, Holy Spirit led way of connecting with God. It should always be done with God honoring motives, because if it done with the wrong motives, it will do more harm than good—it will become a form of idolatry in itself.

Satan and his evil forces are at work in the world; and in aspects of faith, Christian teachings have become distorted, and false teachers and false belief systems have been tools that Satan has used to do this. Satan often zones in on topics like God's authority and tell lies about God's triune identity; also, Satan plays down the roles of faith and grace in the Gospel and makes many people think that they have to be 'good enough' to be saved, casting aside Jesus' actions and His ability to completely save them.

In addition, Satan likes to lure people into thinking that they should live for the moment and that they deserve to be the lord of their own lives. He often sweeps spiritual matters 'under the rug' by instilling perverse thoughts in people's minds—thoughts like these: their lives are totally in their control; seeing is believing; science and evolutionary theories provide the answers to life's big questions;

Christian teachings are imaginary religious beliefs that are mostly based on human opinions; Santa Claus and the Easter Bunny are worth worshipping; and heaven, hell, himself, and God do not exist.

Satan also likes to play down the impact of sin and twist the truth in a clever way that gets people in all sorts of trouble—just like he did with Adam and Eve. He leads people down dark, sinful paths and then makes them feel bad about it. He is sly, snide, and extremely dangerous. We do not have to look very far before we can see how broken the world is and how much of a terrible impact evil is having.

But if we are living on God's side, there is no need to fear because He 'has' put and 'will' put the record straight. God is the only God and there is only one Gospel. God is not to be messed with and His teachings never go out of date. He is very much alive, in power, and ever faithful to His promises; and in the future, justice will be done and His dominion will be made known to all people, whether they have believed in Him or not.

THE LINE OF COMMUNICATION

Prayer is simply communicating with God. It is such an honor to be able to openly communicate with God—the Creator of the whole universe—whenever and wherever we want to. God is always available and is always listening. People can ask Him for anything—nothing is ever too big, too small, or too hard for Him to do.

Prayer is powerful, and God answers prayers in His perfect timing and in His perfect ways, although His answers are not always liked, understood, or expected. In prayer, it is good practice to declare how amazing God is, thank Him for His blessings, and ask Him for things—including His forgiveness for the times when we act immorally.

Communicating to God can also be done in the form of singing, which is usually done through singing Bible-based hymns and songs. Believers often pray and sing together, and this tends to be in church settings.

Believers are encouraged to pray for others—including their enemies—and doing so opens the door wider for God's power to go to work, bringing more of His blessings and benefits into people's lives.

Believers tend to pray to the 'Father' although their prayers could be said to 'God' or other members of the Godhead in relation to their specific roles. Prayers tend to draw to a close with phrases such as, 'In Jesus' name' (to recognize that it is Jesus who has enabled the prayers to reach the Father) and 'Amen' (in affirmation to what has been said and to signify the end of the prayers).

When communicating with God, it is important to be respectful, natural, and honest, as well as being ready and open to receive from Him. God can speak to believers in many ways, such as through gut feelings, mental pictures, dreams, words, phrases, objects, people, or Bible verses. Often, He speaks to believers in subtle ways, so it is important that believers are focused on Him in their prayers in order to receive the fullness of His message and more clearly sense what He wants them to know and do.

God likes to hear from His believers because He cares about them. He encourages them to 'pray without ceasing'[15]—in other words, to pray throughout each day. Prayers do not have to be particularly well-planned out or only said on special occasions: they can be as short or as long as feels appropriate and they can be said whenever feels appropriate.

Like any relationship, communication is key; and to communicate with God, and form a strong, loving relationship with Him, prayer is key. Prayer enables believers to know God personally rather than simply knowing about God, and prayer should be the first 'port of call' in all situations. It is extremely beneficial for believers to incorporate prayer into other practices such as studying the Bible, going to church, fasting, and so on.

As believers pray, they will become stronger in their faith, more aware of God's desires for them, and better equipped to serve God with boldness. Prayer is essential when it comes to believers living faithfully, and their time spent communicating with God is certainly time well spent.

THE BIBLE

The Bible is like an instruction manual for life. It consists of a range of different books that include stories, facts, poems, parables, prophecies, songs, and letters, all of which share the very words of God—the Word of Truth.

From start to finish—from the book of Genesis to the book of Revelation—the Bible could be described as one big story about the redemption of God's people, with Christ and the cross as the center of it all. To put it another way, the Bible is about the way in which the relationship worked, works, and will work, between God and all of His creation. Topics about creation, sin, the Savior, and receiving salvation are all covered.

God carefully chose certain people to write the Bible, and He blessed them with the ability to capture the most important messages throughout the entire world's history, no less. The Bible has many authors, but, in a way, God is the only Author because He is the One who gave the authors the very words to write—through the divine inspiration of the Holy Spirit.

There are places in the Bible where Jesus is referred to as 'the Word'[16] and the 'Author of Life'.[17] These names emphasize the amount of power within the Bible and the amazing privilege we have of being able to read It.

As well as practices like prayer, building a stronger relationship with God involves studying the Bible diligently. This is because doing so broadens our understanding of God's nature and provides guidance on what is good and evil, right and wrong, and how to live life to the fullest—in a way that loves, deeply respects, and gladly serves Him.

The Bible is a Book like no other: It is alive and active and a weapon of warfare for Christians. The Word of God is given the title as 'the Sword of the Spirit'.[18] Its powerful content cuts straight to the core of the most important aspects of life. It defeats evil, breaks bondages, and opens up hearts to receive the Gospel.

As believers immerse themselves in the Bible, and seek to hear from God through It, they will learn how to live in a way that is more honorable to God; for instance, they will grow in faith and godly wisdom and will witness the Holy Spirit highlighting certain parts of the Scriptures that strike a chord within them—Scriptures that are relevant to their circumstances and, when learned and applied, will impact their lives in remarkable ways.

The Old Testament part of the Bible contains books that are mainly based on the events that took place between the earth's creation and the time just before Jesus came onto the earth. Whereas, the New Testament part of the Bible contains books that are mainly based on Jesus' life, the growth of the Christian Church, and future times.

It is important for Christians still to learn from the whole Bible and not just the New Testament. This is because the Old and New Testament include events, covenants, promises, and prophesies that relate to one another and are intricately connected; and as believers study the whole of the Bible, they can gain a deeper and richer understanding on how God orchestrates the redemption of His people and how He fits His plans together.

The authenticity of the Bible is second to none. There have been thousands of artifacts found over the years that provide evidence that the stories and written accounts are genuine and show that they match up with other historical events at those times. The Bible has stood firm ever since Its inception, and It is both the best-selling Book and the most read Book of all time.

It is important for Christians that the sacred teachings of the Bible are protected, studied, applied, and preached, because doing these things strengthen existing believers in their faith, bring more people to faith, and give glory to God. The Bible is more than a mere book to Christians: It contains the 'Food' that feeds their souls and the Message that gives life in its fullness.

If you are exploring Christianity, and if you want to start reading the Bible, the books Matthew, Mark, Luke, and John are particularly good places to start; these are called the Gospels, and in these books, Jesus' life on earth is recorded. Other books, like Psalms, Proverbs, and Paul's letters to early churches—such as Philippians and Ephesians—are excellent resources that can help you gain a solid understanding of key Christian principles.

THE CHURCH

The word 'Church' has a several meanings: one meaning refers to the collective family of Jesus' followers, and the other refers to the buildings where believers gather to worship God; therefore, when someone accepts Jesus Christ as the Lord and Savior, they automatically become a member of the Church, and may very well go to a local church in their community.

The main purpose of the local church is to worship God. Other key purposes include leading more people to God, administering sacraments—namely baptism and Holy Communion—supporting existing members in their faith, and serving God in the world by doing good deeds with love, all in the name of the Lord Jesus Christ, giving Him glory.

There are several different types of churches that interpret certain parts of the Bible differently—especially concerning topics like baptism and the gifts of the Holy Spirit. It is important for believers to go to a church where they feel God's presence, where they feel safe, where they grow in faith, and where they believe in the specific teachings being taught.

However, whichever church believers decide to go to, it is of paramount importance that they go to one where fundamental Bible-based teachings—such as the Trinity, the Gospel, and Jesus' identity as truly God and truly man—are behind the sermons they hear, the songs they sing, the prayers they pray, and the deeds they do. This is because there are many places claiming to be Christian places of worship that alter or avoid these fundamental teachings and lead many people astray. People seeking God should stay well clear of these places.

Moreover, the Bible contains God's holy standards and almighty power, and for Him to be glorified, and for the Gospel to serve Its purpose—of transforming lives and saving souls—within a church congregation, His Word cannot be avoided or altered in any way. Faith in God comes by hearing the Word of God, and churches should always strive to preach and apply the Scriptures in a way that supports the Church as a whole, glorifies God, and spreads the good news that the forgiveness of sins has been graciously made available through faith in Jesus Christ.

THE QUESTION

As previously mentioned, life has two main paths: people can turn from their sins, trust God, and believe that Christ has paid the price of their sins and has cleared them from condemnation, or they can reject God, remain as they are, and face the ramifications of rejecting Him.

Often, people are reluctant to turn to God and trust in Him because they feel unworthy of a loving relationship with Him; they can feel as if they have made too many mistakes, do not know enough of the Bible, or that God will not accept them if they were to go to Him. The truth is, we all are unworthy of a loving relationship with God due to our sinful nature—which we inherited from the Fall in the Garden of Eden—and regardless of how much we study the Bible or lead good lives, we can never know enough or do enough to earn a loving relationship with God or our salvation.

The Gospel is the Gospel of grace; Its benefits are totally undeserved and that is what makes It so good. Only Jesus lived perfectly—in a way that warranted God's acceptance. It is important to know that He came to save sinners, not perfect people.

There are many other factors that can prevent people from following God: for example, people may not want to accept that they are sinners; they may not want to give up certain things they are idolizing; they may see wanting a loving relationship with God as a weakness; they may think they do not need God; they may see Christianity as unreal, irrelevant, or outdated; they may be scared to be different from those around them; they may try and live on their terms for as long as they can before turning to God; they may have a distorted perception of who God is, what He is like, and what a faith-filled life looks like; and, they may be deceived into thinking that as long as they are living morally 'good enough' lives they do not have to take Christianity, God, and His teachings very seriously in order to receive salvation.

There will not be anyone on Judgment Day who is mocked for having faith in the Lord. The Bible says that, 'Anyone who believes in Him will never be put to shame'.[19]

To many people, Christianity is viewed as simply an optional sort of self-help strategy to make a believer's struggles more bearable or as a side-hobby to keep them busy. These concepts grossly disrespect God and devalue who He is and what Christ gave His life for.

Christianity is a call from death into Life, a call into the Light, and a call into a loving relationship with our Maker. All of existence revolves around God; He is who He is, yet so often people play down His importance, refuse to believe in Him, or try and make Him into who they want Him to be—in a way that makes them feel more comfortable about living on their own terms, rather than His.

God's 'terms and conditions' are 'set in stone' so to speak—just like how the Ten Commandments were literally written on stone tablets by His mighty hand. The same rules apply to all; everyone will be judged against God's Word, and whoever rejects His Word will still be judged by It.

God certainly knows more than we do; He invented life and His teachings are written for our benefit, even if we do not agree or understand how they will help us—this is where trusting in His wisdom, power, and goodness is required in order to receive salvation and experience significant breakthroughs in our lives.

Seeing what we can gain through trusting in God can really put things in perspective; for instance, here are the sorts of things that get exchanged: worry for peace, weakness for strength, defeat for victory, fear for faith, darkness for light, sin for godliness, and ultimately death for life.

Furthermore, God is not how many people envisage Him to be—a strict head teacher figure who is ready and waiting to punish everyone who steps out of line. Although God does show His anger against sin, and punish those who rebel against Him, He is merciful to whoever goes to Him in repentance and believes in the Gospel of Jesus Christ; these people will be warmly embraced, accepted as His child, and—through their faith—will be continually led along the path that leads to eternal life.

A wonderful thing about the Gospel is that salvation is free. God's overwhelming grace, mercy, love, and compassion for His people cover their multitude of sins and human limitations. And when the time comes, when believers have to stand before God, instead of punishing them, He will show them mercy because He will be able to see that throughout their Christian lives they have sought to please Him and most importantly that they have placed their faith in His beloved Son—who has interceded for them.

The Gospel only bears good news to those who believe; for everyone else it bears extremely bad news—news that they will die in their sins without being forgiven by God. The Gospel, depending on whether It is believed or denied, either brings hope or helplessness, justification or justice, compassion or condemnation, deliverance or destruction. The Gospel offends multitudes of people and It is extremely hard-hitting; none of us like to hear and have to admit that we are sinners and need a Savior. The gravity of what God has done through Christ and the cross heals and hurts on many different levels.

What do you think about Jesus Christ? Some people may think He was simply a good teacher; others may think that He was a liar or even a lunatic. Some may even go so far as thinking that all of Christianity is a big farce or nothing more than a bunch of old fairy tales; however, there is an overwhelming amount of evidence that speaks otherwise: as well as all the physical evidence that has been found—such as the biblical scrolls—there are multitudes of people over the centuries that can testify how much of a profound impact the revelation of the Gospel and their loving relationships with God have had on their lives personally; they have tasted the sweetness of God's grace.

If Jesus is the 'Real Deal' (the Son of God, God in the flesh) and if He did what He said He did and what the evidence suggests He did (defeating death, evil, and the power of sin for His believers) then the destination of each of our eternal futures depend on whether we believe in Him and base our lives around Him or not.

We cannot escape that, at some point in time, we all must stand in front of God and be accountable for what we have done with the lives we have been blessed with here on earth. Faith in Jesus Christ is the only way to have peace with God and it is the only way to obtain the fulfillment in life that we all deeply long for.

The type of personal relationship you have with God is of supreme importance—it is literally a matter of life and death. During Jesus' ministry, He commanded people to 'repent and believe in the Gospel'.[20] To this day, Jesus' command has not changed, and the big question remains: *How will you respond?*

THE TRANSFORMATION

Once believers have committed their lives to Christ, their transformation from their previous way of life to a holy life is unique and personal between them and God. Believers work in partnership with the Holy Spirit who lives in them. He teaches and transforms them in manageable steps to help them serve God effectively and succeed in carrying out His will. The Holy Spirit purifies them over time in a process called 'sanctification'.

Being able to live in a way that honors God does not happen overnight or happen automatically; it is an ongoing developmental process in this life. Believers who are born-again still will fall short of God's standards due to their original sinful human nature; however, the Holy Spirit will help them do what is right, and God will forgive their wrongs, as long as they play their part by consistently pursuing holiness by turning from their sins and applying their faith in Christ.

Although salvation is a free gift for believers—thanks to Christ— their spiritual maturity, sanctification, and obtaining the most fruitful lives that God has for them, comes with a 'COST'; it requires these things from them, which are all closely linked: *commitment*, *obedience*, *sacrifice*, and most importantly *trust*:

- *Committing* their lives to God,

- *Obeying* God's instructions and teachings,

- *Sacrificing* the things that detract them from God,

- *Trusting* in God, with Jesus Christ as their Lord, placing their faith and hope in Him.

Many people see the Christian lifestyle as a boring, rigid way of life, following endless rules resentfully, but this not this case—or definitely should not be the case for a believer. A Christian, Bible-based life trusting in God is an ongoing adventure full of love, hope, peace, joy, power, purpose, surprises... and the list goes on.

When a believer has a solid understanding of what Jesus has done for them, and when they have given their lives to God, they do not change their lifestyle begrudgingly: they change their lifestyle because they want to please God and because the Holy Spirit reveals to them how great God is. Moreover, believers want to show God their gratitude, reciprocate His love, respect Him, and worship Him; and in return, through their faithful obedience, He blesses them with fulfilling lives that are incomparable to their former lifestyles—lives where they can experience and share His love, and learn to be content, irrespective of their circumstances.

This being said, becoming a Christian does not mean that life suddenly becomes a 'walk in the park'; there certainly will be an abundance of blessings and new opportunities, but alongside these comes plenty of opponents, temptations, and key lessons to learn. Believers who truly 'live for Christ' will face persecution for their faith in some way, and being made into the likeness of Christ requires sharing in His suffering—to some degree—and holding fast to His teachings.

Believers are taught to always trust God and be faithful in their tests and trials—even to the point of rejoicing in them—because these hardships refine them and serve as blessings. Through their patience, perseverance, and fearless confidence in God, believers will become better representatives of His Kingdom, and they will be richly rewarded—thanks to His grace.

The Bible states that 'the gate is narrow and the way is difficult that leads to life' (and few people find it), whereas 'the gate is wide and the way is easy that leads to destruction' (and many people enter through it).[21] Believers are taught to 'fight the good fight of the faith'[22] and to 'strip off every weight and every sin that holds them back and to run with endurance the race that set out for them'.[23]

It is important that believers, after giving their lives to God, do not adopt a flippant mindset, thinking that their salvation now gives them a 'free pass' to sit back, relax, and sin as much as their selfish nature desires. Jesus has saved them so that they can do good works, glorify Him, and enjoy their relationship with Him. He has done the impossible for them; they are to carry out God's plans by going 'all in' with Him, consistently seeking Him, submitting to Him, and seizing the opportunities He graciously provides them with.

Some professing Christians choose to settle for less than God's best, and then they can even stoop so low as to then blame Him for their circumstances; they can be resentful towards God rather counting their blessings and remembering that Christians have a responsibility to live in a way that reflects their salvation and serves Him reverently (with deep respect).

God knows the desires of people's hearts and knows exactly who the members of His family are. Whether or not someone is saved is not for us to judge. It does not matter if people have been going to a church their whole lives, or if they appear on the surface to be saints rather than sinners, they may deep down be swamped in sin and be living to please themselves rather than God. On the flip side, if people appear immature in their faith, and appear to have a lot of sin in their lives, it does not necessarily mean they are not saved—God may still be at work within them.

It is important to know that there is no such thing as a genuine Christian who continues to live carnally—without showing any fruits of the Spirit—once they are born-again; people will obey God's teachings if they truly love God—it is as simple as that. Jesus said that His disciples (His followers) will continue in His Word.[24] The Word of God certainly works and the Holy Spirit helps Christians become more holy.

To build believers up, test their faith, and train them up in righteousness, God sets up challenges for them; but however hard, harsh, insignificant, or crazy these challenges may seem, God is the best Teacher and He always provides believers with the resilience and resources they need to do His will when they rely on Him—He works all things out for those who love Him.[25]

Believers will be blessed from their obedience in one way or another; whatever they do for God is never done in vain.[26] It is faith along with the power of the Holy Spirit that both fuel the sanctifying journey that believers go on with God. And on this journey, believers will be continually shown what really matters in life—and how to get the most out of it—and God will give them the grace to become all that they were created to be.

Living by faith rather than sight ironically allows believers to see things in their lives clearer. The Spirit lights up their souls as well as guides their steps. They are given the 'Light of Life'[27] and are collectively—with other members of the Church—assigned the task of brightening up the world.

The Christian life is by no means a trouble-free, easy life without worries or strife—this world we live in is still broken, sin-ridden, and ruled by Satan—but life is a whole lot better with God than it is without Him: the Christian life is a life of faith, hope, love, forgiveness, redemption, and victory over evil; and the Christian life has peace with God, along with His constant protection and provision, not to mention the security of eternal life to look forward to.

If you are stuck in a rut, feel lost, and are looking for something meaningful to hope in and live for... there is good news. If you are fed up of following the wicked ways of this world and want to make a new start... there is good news. If you feel weighed down by a deep sense of restlessness and feel guilty because of your sins... there is good news.

And here it is: God is ready to forgive you, guard you, guide you, and give you a new identity as His child if... (1) you believe that Jesus Christ is the Lord your God—who lovingly died on the cross for you —and (2) you are willing to humbly turn to God in repentance and follow Him with all of your heart.

He will save you. He will transform you. He will set you free.

Do you believe? And are you willing?

To profess your faith in Jesus Christ as your Lord and Savior and become a child of the Living God, you can say our prayer in the next section; and if you would like to learn more about aspects of living a faith-filled life, you can visit our website: ImmanuelMinistries.org

Also, you may be interested in reading our book called 'Be Strong and Courageous as a Child of God.'

THE PRAYER

Dear God,

I'm so sorry for my sinful past; I now come to Your throne.

I ask that You take control of my life; my old way of living, I disown.

I believe You are the Father, the Holy Spirit, and the Son.

I believe Jesus Christ is my Lord and Savior, and I believe in all He's done:

I believe He took away my sins and died on the cross to save me;

I believe He rose on the third day and will reign for eternity.

I ask that You forgive me and help me learn and grow in Your ways.

I believe You made me, love me, and will be with me for all my days.

I thank You for accepting me; I look forward to my new life with You.

I desire to honor You in my thoughts and words, and in everything I do.

In Jesus' name, I pray, Amen.

If you have just made this commitment, congratulations. Immanuel Ministries would like you to have our 'New Believer's Blessing' document. You can find this on our website on our Free Downloads page:

immanuelministries.org/free-downloads

THE REFERENCES

1. Exodus 20:1-17
2. Matthew 3:2
3. Matthew 3:17 BSB
4. Matthew 5:28 BSB
5. Matthew 5:22
6. Mark 12:30 BSB
7. Mark 12:31 BSB
8. John 19:30
9. Revelation 5:12
10. Revelation 5:5
11. Romans 10:9 BSB
12. John 14:6
13. John 6:63 BSB
14. 1 Corinthians 6:9-10
15. 1 Thessalonians 5:17
16. John 1:14
17. Acts 3:15
18. Ephesians 6:17
19. Romans 10:11 BSB
20. Mark 1:15
21. Matthew 7:13-14
22. 1 Timothy 6:12 BSB
23. Hebrews 12:1
24. John 8:31
25. Romans 8:28
26. 1 Corinthians 15:58
27. John 8:12

THE PUBLISHER

At Immanuel Ministries, we share the good news of the Gospel with people—the news that they can be forgiven of their sins, have peace with God, and live a victorious life in union with Him forever through loving, believing, and following Jesus Christ.

Visit our website if you would like to learn more:
ImmanuelMinistries.org

Feel free to contact us via email:
contact@immanuelministries.org

God bless you.

Printed in Great Britain
by Amazon